HISTORIC
COMMUNITIES

Fort Life

Bobbie Kalman and David Schimpky

Crabtree Publishing Company

HISTORIC
COMMUNITIES

Created by Bobbie Kalman

For my parents

Editor-in-Chief
Bobbie Kalman

Writing team
Bobbie Kalman
David Schimpky

Editors
Tammy Everts
Lynda Hale
Petrina Gentile

Research
David Schimpky
Lori Pattenden

Consultant
Dennis Farmer

Computer design
Lynda Hale

Illustrations
Tammy Everts: pages 9, 12, 21, 25, 29
Antoinette "Cookie" DeBiasi: cover design, page 28
Barb Bedell: cover

Color separations
Book Art Inc.

Printer
Worzalla Publishing

Special thanks to: Kevin Young, Anthony Saez, Rebecca Eisenbarth, Marty Mascarin, Chuck Dale, Debby Padgett, Rosemary Frey, and the staff of Fort George: Erin O'Farrell, Doug McRae, Chris Zoetewey, Daniel Griffin, Russ Noble, Jill Plitnikas, Kyle Upton, Alex Dale, Jozef Tkaczyk, and Michael Allen

Title page: A sentry stands guard at the gate of the fort at Jamestown, Virginia.

Published by
Crabtree Publishing Company

350 Fifth Avenue	360 York Road, RR 4	73 Lime Walk
Suite 3308	Niagara-on-the-Lake	Headington
New York	Ontario, Canada	Oxford OX3 7AD
N.Y. 10118	L0S 1J0	United Kingdom

Cataloging in Publication Data
Kalman, Bobbie, 1947-
    Fort life

(The historic communities series)
Includes index.
ISBN 0-86505-496-7 (library bound)   ISBN 0-86505-516-5 (pbk.)
The historic forts of North America and the lifestyles of the men, women, and children who lived there are highlighted in this book.

1. Fortification - North America - Juvenile literature. 2. Frontier and pioneer life - North America - Juvenile literature.
I. Schimpky, David, 1969-   . II. Title.   III. Series: Kalman, Bobbie, 1947-   . Historic communities.

UG413.K35 1994   j355.7'0971   LC 93-39881

Contents

4   A protected community

7   Early forts

8   The fort garrison

12   Life in the barracks

14   Officers' quarters

16   Drilling

19   Music

21   Guarding the fort

22   Food for the soldier

24   The infirmary

26   Other buildings

28   A tale of two forts

30   The fort today

31   Glossary

32   Index and photo credits

A protected community

In Europe, it is common to see walled cities and huge castles that were once important **fortifications**. Fortifications are defenses, such as banked-up earth, rough logs, or thick stone, that make something strong. The first Europeans to settle in North America brought the tradition of building fortifications with them.

A special protected area was called a **fort**. Forts served many purposes. Some were outposts for soldiers; others were places to do business; still others were places of safety for settlers. No matter how different they were, all forts had one thing in common—they were strong!

Strong defenses

Fort walls were constructed from wood or stone. Wooden walls, called **stockades**, were made of upright poles. Stone walls were stronger than wooden walls but took longer to build.

Sometimes earth was shaped into walls or used to make walls stronger. These **earthworks** absorbed cannon fire, whereas wooden or stone walls would break and the flying pieces could injure people. A deep ditch, which lined the outside of the walls, made it difficult for enemy soldiers to approach the fort.

*(right) Jamestown was one of North America's first forts. (inset) This eighteenth-century etching shows Fort-Saint-Frédéric in Crown Point, New York. At each corner of the fort, you can see **bastions**. These structures allowed soldiers to shoot enemy soldiers who were right up against the fort walls.*

The walls of homes in Jamestown were made of woven branches that were coated with hard mud. This type of construction is called **wattle and daub.** *The roofs were thatched with straw.*

Early forts

When the first European settlers came to what is now the United States and Canada, they built forts. These simple log structures provided shelter and defense. The settlers farmed fields outside the forts, growing enough food to last through the long winters.

Why build a fort?

The early settlements needed to be defended. Some, such as the English settlement in Jamestown, Virginia, feared attacks from Native groups who did not welcome the newcomers. For others, there was a greater danger of attack from other settlements. An early French settlement in what is now St. Augustine, Florida, was destroyed by Spanish adventurers. The Habitation, another French settlement in what is now Nova Scotia, was attacked by settlers from Jamestown who sailed up the coast.

There were no armies at these forts. The forts were defended by the settlers themselves. Special days were set aside for training the male colonists in military skills.

Fur forts

Some forts were places of business. Fur-trading forts were built across North America during the seventeenth, eighteenth, and nineteenth centuries. Many of these forts became military outposts, and some grew into communities. Fort-Pontchartrain du Détroit, which was built on the shores of the Detroit River, is now the city of Detroit, Michigan.

When a canoe fleet loaded down with furs arrived at a fort, the trading began with an elaborate ritual. The head of the canoe fleet exchanged gifts with the head trader, and both marched with much ceremony to the local settlement.

The clerk was an important part of the fur-fort community. He was responsible for recording how many furs were received from trappers. The fur trappers traded the pelts for items such as tools and guns.

The fort garrison

(top) Before armies were formed in North America, settlers banded together to form military units called **militias**. Originally, militias protected local communities. Later, they provided extra soldiers in times of war. Sometimes militia troops were stationed at forts. (inset) Soldiers in the **artillery** were responsible for loading, aiming, and firing the cannons.

The most common type of fort was the military fort. These forts defended such important places as harbors, rivers, roads, and cities. The group of people who lived in a military fort was called a **garrison**. The garrison included regular soldiers, officers, women, and children. Like other forts, military forts were a type of community. The inside of the fort, with its many buildings, was like a small town.

Every person in the fort, from the commanding officer to the person who cleaned the stables, had a job to do.

Regular soldiers

Most people in the army joined, or **enlisted**, as a career. They were known as regular soldiers, or **enlisted men**. Some volunteered so they would not have to go to prison; some wanted the glory of battle; others joined because they could find no other work.

saber

(left) Most soldiers were in the **infantry.** *They had to fight on foot, using weapons such as muskets, rifles, and* **bayonets.**
(right) The **cavalry** *rode on horseback and fought with swords, called* **sabers,** *and guns.*

Officers

Officers were responsible for supervising the men. Until the middle of the nineteenth century, most officers in the British army came from wealthy families. Some bought their rank; others achieved it because they knew the right people. In the American army, most officers had the same background, but there was more opportunity for ordinary soldiers to get promoted. Eventually, promotions in both armies were based on a soldier's experience and ability. Many officers were trained at special military academies.

The commanding officer

The commanding officer carried full responsibility for the fort and the soldiers in his charge. His duties included reporting to his superior officers, planning patrols and watches, and supervising the soldiers. The commanding officer was usually assisted by another officer called an **aide**.

Women and children

Most garrisons included some women and children. Sometimes officers brought their wives and children to the fort, where they lived comfortably. The families of some enlisted men lived at the fort as well. The wives were given jobs such as working in the kitchen and doing laundry. This work was very hard. Children worked too. They cleaned horse stalls, made candles, and helped in the kitchen.

(top) Laundry duties were usually assigned to women.
(middle) It was very important to show respect to officers.
(bottom) Officers enjoyed active social lives.
(opposite page) Boys were often trained as musicians.

Life in the barracks

The barracks were home to the soldiers and, occasionally, their wives and children, too. At larger forts, hundreds of people lived together in the barracks. They ate, slept, and spent their leisure time there. The large rooms were filled with beds, tables, and benches.

No place like home

Not only were the barracks home to the soldiers—they were also home to numerous rats and mice. The smell was extremely unpleasant because soldiers rarely had the opportunity to bathe. Many soldiers felt that the worst part of life in the barracks was the lack of privacy. There was never a moment to be alone.

(top) Although the barracks were crowded and often dirty, they were also lively places. Many of the soldiers became friends for life.

Bedtime

The soldiers usually slept on straw mattresses and covered themselves with woolen blankets and, sometimes, sheets. Often, two or three soldiers had to share a bed. Soldiers also shared their beds with a variety of insects, which spread many diseases. The senior enlisted men, such as sergeants and corporals, had first choice of beds. They usually picked a bed near the fireplace or stove in winter and near the window in summer. The men kept their personal belongings in their packs or in small trunks at the end of their beds.

Time to relax

The lives of soldiers were difficult. Their days were filled with hard work and little rest. As a result, they looked forward to leisure time in the evenings. The soldiers told stories to one another, drank their daily ration of beer or whiskey or, if they lived at a large fort, read a book from the garrison library. Gambling was a favorite pastime, although some soldiers lost their wages —and even their uniforms—in card games. For this reason, many forts did not permit gambling.

Sunday morning

Attending religious services was considered an important part of a soldier's life. If a soldier missed a service, he could lose a portion of his pay or even spend time in jail! On Sunday morning the soldiers went to the fort chapel. If the fort had no chapel, the soldiers put on their dress uniforms and marched to a local church.

(top) Soldiers and their wives managed to have a bit of privacy by hanging a blanket around their bed.
(middle) Soldiers needed to have good card-playing skills!
(bottom) The barracks were filled with wooden bunks.

Officers' quarters

The officers' quarters were much better than those of the ordinary soldiers. Their homes were often luxurious and filled with fine furniture. If an officer was married, his wife and children lived with him in his quarters, although, in many cases, the family lived in a nearby town. At very large forts there were special houses for officers and their families.

Relaxing

Officers had much more leisure time than the regular soldiers did. Much of this time was spent in the officers' gamesroom. This room was equipped with card-playing tables, chessboards, and backgammon sets. Many officers were well educated and enjoyed reading. Some spent their leisure time hunting and fishing.

Dinner is served

Officers ate very well. They enjoyed big meals of fresh meat, including venison, goose, rabbit, lamb, beef, or pork, depending on what was available. Fine wines and delicious pastries accompanied the meals.

Keeping a servant

Most officers had servants. **Batmen**, or **officer's orderlies,** were personal servants taken from among the enlisted men. Officers who had their family living in the fort sometimes hired young women as maids. Unfortunately, these servants were difficult to keep! Soon after they were hired, the women left their jobs to marry the soldiers they met in the fort.

(above) Officers were responsible for planning drills and patrols. (opposite page, top) A batman's duties included cleaning and polishing boots, taking care of the officer's uniform, and keeping the officer's quarters clean and warm. (opposite page, bottom) The officers ate their meals in the officers' mess, a dining room that was located in their quarters. Officers' meals were often splendid occasions, complete with silverware and fine china.

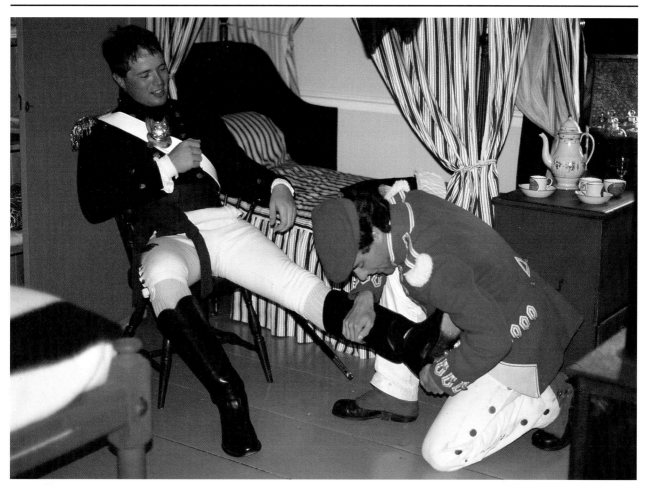

Drilling

In the middle of the fort was a large open area called the **parade ground**. It was the site of most of the drilling and troop assemblies.

The daily routine

Soldiers had to drill in pouring rain, blazing heat, and freezing cold. They hated this part of their daily routine. The purpose of frequent drilling was to teach the soldiers to perform certain tasks without thinking. The drills were led by the sergeant, who could be very impatient with the soldiers in his charge. It was not uncommon to hear the sergeant give a sloppy soldier a good tongue-lashing.

Arms drills

One important drill was **musket** loading. The musket was a type of gun used until the 1840s. It could fire only one shot at a time and had to be reloaded quickly. The soldiers practiced loading so often that it became an automatic skill.

Hup, two, three, four!

Marching drills were also important. When in battle, the soldiers had to march quickly and in an orderly fashion to signals beaten on a drum. When muskets were in use, the soldiers stood shoulder to shoulder on the battlefield and fired **volleys** at the enemy. The enemy faced a deadly flurry of hundreds of lead balls. Standing shoulder to shoulder made it difficult for enemy soldiers to break through the line. This and other formations were practiced over and over again to make sure that the soldiers would not make mistakes in battle.

Military training was part of life for settlers at Jamestown.

Bayonets were blades that attached to the end of a musket or rifle. Drills taught soldiers to "fix bayonets" quickly and use them effectively in battle.

(above) The cavalry performed drills on horseback. Some horses were so used to the routines that they continued the drills even after their riders fell off!
(right) Soldiers had to assemble in an orderly fashion.
(below) Drilling taught soldiers skills that they would need during battles.

Music

Some soldiers were trained as musicians. Drummers, many of whom were young boys, provided a steady beat for drills and marches. In the War of Independence and the War of 1812, drummers gave signals during the battles. The bugler was extremely important during the nineteenth century. During battles, bugle calls were used as signals for charges and retreats. The bugler woke the fort early in the morning with the **reveille**. A mournful tune called **taps** was played on the bugle in the evening and at the funerals of fallen soldiers.

(above) Bagpipes were used by Scottish units in the British army.
(top left) The sound of the fife, a simple instrument similar to a flute, accompanied soldiers on long marches.
(top right) Bugle calls were a vital way of sending messages to soldiers during battles.
(opposite page) The drummer was often a young man who was not yet old enough to be a soldier.

(above) Cavalry patrols were sent from the fort to look for signs of trouble.

(left) All visitors to the fort had to report to the sentry. Sometimes a password was required to enter!

(below) The jail was located in the guardhouse. Constructed of thick wood or stone, the jail cells were dark, damp, and cold.

Guarding the fort

It was very important that the fort be strong and secure. The **guardhouse** was a small building in the fort that was the center of **sentry** operations and other security matters.

Standing on guard

Sentries were soldiers assigned to guard the fort. They paraded around the top of the walls, walked outside the fort, or stood at the gate, keeping a sharp eye out for signs of trouble or enemy activity. There were sentries on duty 24 hours a day. The night watches were the least popular. Sometimes tired sentries fell asleep, only to wake up to the kick of an angry officer. The unfortunate sentry who slept on duty faced harsh discipline.

Doing time

It was very important that soldiers follow orders and do their jobs well. Otherwise, the garrison would not be able to co-operate during a battle, and lives might be lost. If an enlisted man committed a crime or failed to carry out an order, he was punished severely. For offenses such as drunkenness or missing inspection, a typical punishment was loss of pay or a day in jail.

Serious matters

Punishments were very harsh in the British army. Many crimes were punished by whippings, some of which were so bad that they caused death. Very serious crimes, such as desertion, mutiny, or striking an officer, could be punished with death. In the American army, these crimes were usually punished with prison and hard labor.

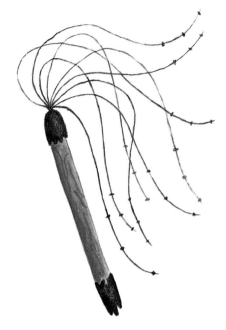

The **cat-o'-nine-tails** *whip was a brutal punishment tool used by the British army.*

Kitchen police duty, *or* **K. P. duty,** *was a punishment for minor offenses.*

Food for the soldier

Provisions at the fort had to last a long time. Foods such as salt pork and beef, flour, rice, and peas kept for months. **Hard tack** was a common food eaten by soldiers. This type of biscuit, described by some people as tasting a little like a brick, didn't go bad as quickly as bread. Lemons and limes were eaten to prevent a disease called **scurvy**, which is caused by a lack of vitamin C. If the fort were near a town, the food was much better. Local farmers sold fresh meat, eggs, butter, and vegetables to the fort.

Mealtime

Until the 1870s, most soldiers had to prepare their own food. Small groups of men shared cooking pots and rations. Unfortunately, the meals were not very appetizing. The meat was often rotten, and there was seldom enough to eat.

(opposite page) Many forts had a bakery so the soldiers could have bread each day. The bakers had to work quickly to provide enough bread for everyone.

(below) In some forts, the soldiers ate in a room called the **mess hall***. The mess hall did not get its name because the soldiers were sloppy eaters—the word "mess" comes from an old word that meant "meal."*

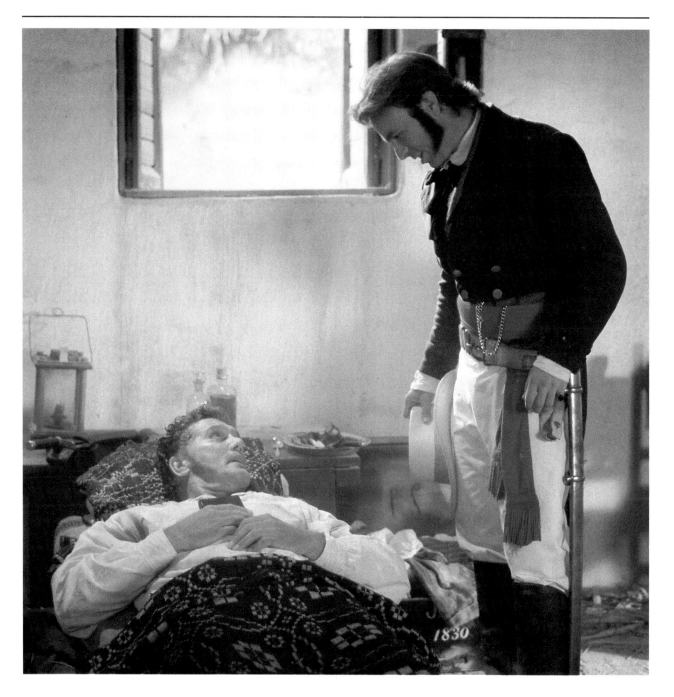

The infirmary

(above) This photograph is from a film depicting the defense of the Alamo. It shows the fort's infirmary. An actor portraying Colonel William Barret Travis, the commanding officer, visits a sick soldier.

Many forts had a small hospital called an infirmary. There was plenty of work for the fort's doctor—diseases were common among the soldiers. Unhealthy foods, unsanitary conditions, and hard work made soldiers weak and often sick. When there were battles, it was the doctor's job to help the wounded.

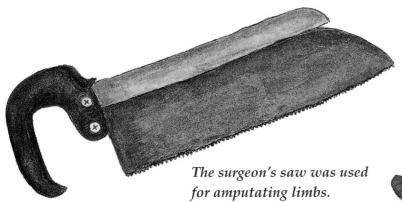

The surgeon's saw was used for amputating limbs.

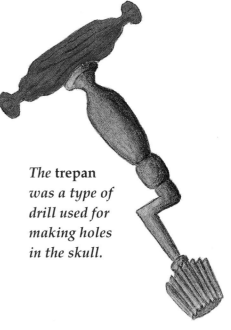

*The **trepan** was a type of drill used for making holes in the skull.*

The doctor

The doctor was not a very popular person in the fort. Medical practices of the day often made a patient's condition worse instead of better. A common cure for many ailments was **bloodletting**. The doctor made a slit in the arm of the patient to let blood out. Usually, this treatment only made patients weaker. Another cure was a spoonful of **blackstrap syrup**, which tasted awful and had no benefit for the soldier. If a doctor felt that he did not have enough skill to help a patient, the sick person was taken for a bumpy ride to the nearest hospital in the back of a wagon. There, if he was still alive, he had a chance to receive better medical care.

Painful remedy

During battle, the doctor had to perform quick surgery. There were no painkillers to help the soldier endure the agony. The most common operation was **amputation**. Limbs were severed from the body if there were badly broken bones, bullet or shrapnel wounds, or frostbite. The surgery was done with a crude saw. Even if the soldier survived the wound and the amputation, he often died of infection because the doctor's hands and tools were dirty.

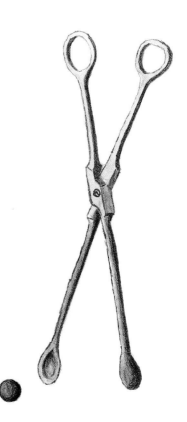

This device was perfect for removing musketballs from the body.

Other buildings

The storehouses

One soldier was assigned to be the **quartermaster**. His duty was to ensure that the fort's storehouses were full of supplies. The quartermaster's job could be a difficult one, especially in a very large fort. Items in the fort's storerooms included weapons, blankets, leather, tools, and food.

The stables

Most forts kept horses, either for officers and cavalry or for hauling wagons, cannons, or plows. The horses were kept in the stables, which had to be cleaned regularly. Cleaning the stable was an unpopular job often assigned to the children at the fort!

The sutler's store

The **sutler** was an important part of the American fort garrison, even though he was not a soldier. The sutler was a civilian who operated a special store for the soldiers. The sutler's store was a favorite place for regular soldiers and officers to visit when they weren't on duty.

(top) A full storeroom was essential, especially if there were a danger of having supplies cut off during a war. (bottom) At the sutler's store, soldiers could spend their pay on a variety of items, including extra food, alcohol, tools, clothes, blankets, and tobacco.

Artisan's workshops

Every fort had artisans who worked in shops. Carpenters were responsible for building and repairing furniture, wagons, and parts of the fort itself. The tailor repaired uniforms, blankets, and flags.

The chapel

Some large forts had chapels within their walls, where a soldier called the **chaplain** conducted religious services. Other duties of the chaplain included visiting sick or wounded soldiers and making sure there were Bibles for the soldiers to read. In some areas, chaplains made efforts to convert the local Native peoples to Christianity.

The powder magazine

The **magazine** was a well-built structure used for storing gunpowder. This building had thick walls of brick or stone to prevent fire. If the magazine caught fire, a huge explosion from the gunpowder could destroy the entire fort. It was also important that the magazine not be damp because it would make the gunpowder useless.

(top) The blacksmith was an artisan who fixed weapons, made tools and horseshoes, and shod horses and oxen. (bottom) This sturdy magazine, made of brick, was used by the militia of Williamsburg, Virginia, for storing weapons and powder.

A tale of two forts

During the War of 1812, the United States fought against Britain and Canada. The purpose of many battles was to capture the enemy's fort. Fort Niagara and Fort George are good examples of why the War of 1812 has been called a "war of forts."

A strategic spot

Fort Niagara was originally a French fur-trading fort, built at the mouth of the Niagara River. It was a good place for a fort because the river was

(above) This picture shows the defenders of Fort Niagara during an artillery battle with Fort George. During the battle, everyone pitched in to help. The woman is taking **hot shot** *from an oven. Hopefully, the red-hot cannonball will hit a wooden building on the other side of the river and cause a fire.*

a major transportation route, connecting Lakes Superior, Michigan, Huron, and Erie to Lake Ontario, the St. Lawrence River, and the Atlantic Ocean. Fort Niagara later became a French military fort but was captured by the British army in 1759. At the end of the War of Independence, Fort Niagara was given to the United States.

Border defense

Across the river from Fort Niagara, Fort George was built by the British between 1796 and 1799. The purpose of this fort was to protect the Canadian border from American attack after the United States became independent from Britain.

Attack on Fort George

On May 27, 1813, American forces attacked Fort George. As infantry troops attacked the fort on land, warships in the river blasted the fort with cannon fire. The raid was a success, and a small American force held Fort George until December, when they abandoned it, burned the nearby town of Newark, and returned to Fort Niagara.

The British strike back

Soon after, the British army moved back into Fort George and used it as a base for a surprise attack on Fort Niagara. The British captured Fort Niagara and held it until the end of the war when, once again, it was given back to the United States. Within 60 years, Fort Niagara had been held by the French, by the British, and by the Americans. Fort George had been occupied by British and American garrisons. No doubt the local villagers wondered who would control these forts next!

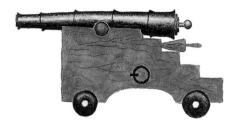

This type of cannon is called a **garrison cannon.** *It could be found in most forts.*

Under attack

The most effective way in which forts were attacked was called a **siege.** During a siege, an army surrounded the fort and tried to smash down its walls with cannon fire. They hoped that the fort inhabitants would give up after their supplies ran out or enough soldiers were killed.

Inside the fort, soldiers busily loaded, aimed, and fired their cannons at the enemy. Other soldiers fired their guns over the fort walls or through narrow slits in the walls. Some hauled cannonballs and gunpowder to the cannons. Damage to the walls was quickly repaired, and any buildings that were on fire were doused with water. Everyone had a job to do— their survival depended on doing it well.

The fort today

It is difficult to find a place in North America that isn't near a fort of some kind. Ask your teacher or a parent where the closest fort to your home or school is. Some forts are still used by the military as places to train soldiers, but most forts are historic sites. Some are in ruins, whereas others look the same as they did centuries ago. Many historic forts offer tours that explain what life was like when the fort was a living community. People in old-fashioned costumes make you feel as if you have gone back in time! You may wish to visit the library to learn more about your local fort and its history.

Write a story about life in a fort and the brave men, women, and children who lived there. Your story might be full of action, adventure, romance, or mystery. You may want to write a scary tale about ghosts at the fort. Perhaps some soldiers never left!

Glossary

ammunition Bullets, musketballs, or cannonballs that are fired from guns

backgammon A type of board game

bugle A type of brass horn

charge A vigorous attack during a battle

civilian Someone who is not a member of the military

colonist Someone who settles in a territory controlled by a distant country

desertion The act of leaving military service without permission

discipline Punishment

dress uniform A uniform worn by soldiers on special occasions

drill An exercise that teaches military skills

fleet A large group of boats or ships

frostbite The condition of having a part of one's body partially frozen

infection An illness spread by germs

mutiny A rebellion of soldiers against officers

provisions Food supplies

rank The level of military authority. For example, colonel is a higher rank than captain; sergeant is a higher rank than private.

rations The amount of food given to soldiers

retreat A movement in which an army leaves a dangerous position and goes back to a safer one

ritual A ceremonial practice

sever To cut off

shod Past tense of the verb "shoe"

shrapnel Metal fragments from an explosive

unsanitary Unclean

venison Deer meat

Index

aide 10

artillery 8, 28

bagpipes 19

baker 22

barracks 12-13

bastions 4

batmen 14

blacksmith 27

bugle 19

cannon 4, 8, 29

carpenter 27

cat-o'-nine-tails 21

cavalry 9, 17, 20

chapel 13, 26

chaplain 27

children 10, 12, 14, 26

church 13

desertion 21

disease 13, 22, 24, 25

doctor 24, 25

drilling 16-17, 19

drum 19

early forts 6-7

earthworks 4

enlisted men 9, 10, 13, 21

fife 19

food 14, 22-23

Fort George 28, 29

Fort Niagara 28, 29

Fort-Pontchartrain du Détroit 7

Fort-Saint-Frédéric 4

fur forts 7, 28

gambling 13

games 13, 14

garrison 8-11

guardhouse 20, 21

Habitation 7

hard tack 22

hot shot 28

infantry 9, 29

infirmary 24-25

jail 13, 20, 21

Jamestown 4, 6, 7

kitchen police duty 21

magazine 27

mess hall 22

military fort 8, 29, 30

militia 8

music 10, 18-19

mutiny 21

Native peoples 7, 27

officers 10, 14, 21, 26

officers' quarters 14-15

punishment 13, 21

quartermaster 26

saber 9

scurvy 22

sentry 20, 21

settlers 7

siege 29

stables 26

stockades 4

storehouses 26

surgery 25

sutler 26

tailor 27

War of 1812 19, 28, 29

War of Independence 19, 29

weapons 4, 8, 9, 16, 27, 28, 29

Williamsburg 27

women 10, 12, 13, 14, 28

Photo credits

Castillo de San Marco National Monument: page 9 (left)

Colonial Williamsburg Foundation: page 8 (top)

Marc Crabtree: pages 11, 13 (all), 17 (top right, bottom), 19 (all), 20 (top left, bottom), 27 (top)

Fort Laramie National Historic Site: pages 12, 20 (top right), 23

Fort Scott National Historic Site: page 9 (right), 10 (bottom), 15 (bottom), 17 (top left), 21, 22, 26 (all), 27 (top)

Jamestown-Yorktown Foundation: title page, pages 4-5, 6, 16 (top)

Bobbie Kalman: pages 10 (middle), 14, 15 (top), 27 (bottom), 30

Old Fort William: page 7 (all)

Parks Canada, Halifax Citadel National Historic Site: pages 10 (top), 16 (bottom), 31

Copyright 1991, Rivertheatre Associates, Ltd., San Antonio, Texas (from the film "Alamo... The Price of Freedom"): pages 8 (inset), 18, 24

Weir Foundation, Queenston, Ontario: page 5 (inset): Proud, *A North View of Fort-Saint-Frédéric on Crown Point*

2 3 4 5 6 7 8 9 0 Printed in U.S.A. 3 2 1 0 9 8 7 6 5 4